Psalm

91

THE ULTIMATE SHIELD

WORLD BIBLE PUBLISHERS, INC.
Iowa Falls, IA 50126 U.S.A.

Psalm 91
THE ULTIMATE SHIELD
for Enduring Protection

© Copyright 2001 by Michael and Brenda Pink
All rights reserved.

Published by:
World Bible Publishers, Inc.
Iowa Falls, IA U.S.A.

*The King James Version was the
primary translation used. Where necessary,
20th Century words or phrases having
the same meaning were substituted by
the author to be more readily
comprehended by today's reader.*

ISBN 1-877994-08-1
ISBN 0-529-11575-1 (camo edition)

Manufactured in the U.S.A.

2 3 4 5 DP 05 04 03 02

DEDICATION

The 91st Psalm has been known throughout the ages as a psalm of protection. In 1991, with that in mind, this book was dedicated to Scott who served as a Marine in Operation Desert Shield/Desert Storm and was called *Psalm 91—The Ultimate Shield.*

During that conflict we received numerous letters from soldiers, some who wrote us during Scud missile attacks, who were finding great comfort and strength from that book. Countless others found and put their trust in Christ.

On September 11th, 2001, when America was struck by terrorist attacks on civilian targets, we knew it was time to re-introduce the book. If we are going to have "Enduring Freedom," we're going to need "Enduring Protection" from God on High.

We dedicate this book to men and women in the cause of freedom everywhere.

"It is for freedom that Christ has set us free."
Galatians 5:1 NIV

Michael & Brenda Pink

TABLE OF CONTENTS

PSALM 91
THE ULTIMATE SHIELD

An Overview

To Whom the Promise is Made:

He that dwells in the secret place of the most High shall abide under the shadow of the Almighty. **Verse 1**

Your Confession:

I will say of the LORD, "He is my refuge and my fortress: my God in Him will I trust." **Verse 2**

The Promise of DELIVERANCE:

Surely He shall deliver you from the snare of the fowler and from the deadly pestilence.

Verse 3

The Promise of PROTECTION:

He shall cover you with His feathers, and under His wings shall you trust and find refuge: His truth and His faithfulness shall be your shield and buckler. **Verse 4**

The Promise of COURAGE:

You will not be afraid of the terror of the night: Nor of the arrow that flies by day: Nor for the pestilence that walks in the darkness; Nor for the destruction that lays waste at noonday.

Verses 5 & 6

The Promise of SAFETY:

A thousand shall fall at your side and ten thousand at your right hand; but it will not come near you. You will only watch with your eyes as you witness the reward of the wicked. **Verses 7 & 8**

The Promise of SECURITY:

Because you have made the LORD your refuge and the Most High your place of dwelling; there shall no evil befall you, neither shall any plague come near your tent. **Verses 9 & 10**

The Promise of HELP:

For He will give His angels charge over you, to keep you in all your ways. They will lift you up in their hands, lest you dash your foot against a stone. **Verses 11 & 12**

The Promise of VICTORY

You will tread upon the lion and the cobra: the young lion and the serpent you will trample under foot. **Verse 13**

The Promise of HONOR

Because he has set his love upon Me, therefore I will deliver him. I will set him on high because he has known My name. He will call upon Me and I will answer him: I will be with him in trouble; I will deliver him, and honor him. **Verses 14 & 15**

The Promise of LIFE:

With long life will I satisfy him, and show him My salvation. **Verse 16**

Chapter 1

TO WHOM THE PROMISE IS MADE

He that dwells in the secret place of the most High shall abide under the shadow of the Almighty. **Verse 1**

LORD, who will dwell in Your tent? Who will live in Your holy hill? He that walks uprightly, and does what is right, speaking the truth from his heart. He that does not slander, nor do wrong to his friend, nor take up a reproach against his neighbor. In whose eyes a vile person is despised: but he honors them that fear the LORD. He keeps his word, even when it hurts and does not change. He lends his money without interest, and does not accept a bribe against the innocent. He who does these things will never be moved.[1]

You are my hiding place and my shield: I hope in Your Word.[2] In the time of trouble You will hide me in Your shelter: in the secret of Your tent You will conceal me: You will set me upon a rock,[3] and hide me in the secret of Your presence from the pride of man.[4]

The secret of the LORD is with them that fear You; and You will show them Your covenant.[5] Oh how great is Your goodness, which you have stored up for them that fear You; which You have brought about for them that trust in You in sight of the sons of men.[6] Be my rock of refuge, my strong shelter, to which I may continually resort: You have given commandment to save me; for You are my rock and my fortress.[7]

The eyes of the LORD are upon the righteous, and His ears are open to their cry.[8] Know that the LORD has set apart him that is godly for Himself: the LORD will hear him when he calls unto Him.[9] So commit your way unto the LORD; trust also in Him; and He will bring it to pass.[10]

Whoever believes in Jesus Christ will not dwell in darkness[11] and whoever confesses that Jesus is the Son of God, God dwells in him, and he dwells in God.[12] Jesus will pray to the Father and He will give you another Comforter, that He may live with you forever; Even the Spirit of truth.[13]

Jesus said, "Dwell in Me, and I will dwell in you. As the branch cannot bear fruit of itself, unless it lives in the vine; neither can you unless you dwell in Me. I am the vine, you are the branches: He that dwells in Me and I in him, the same brings forth much fruit: for without Me you can do nothing. If a man does not dwell in Me, he is cast away as a branch and is withered; and men gather them, and throw them into the fire, and they are burned. If you dwell in Me, and My words dwell in you, you shall ask what you will, and it will be done unto you."[14]

He that keeps His commandments dwells in Him and He in him,[15] and will abide in His love even as Jesus kept His Father's commandments, and abides in His love.[16] In fact, he that continues in the teachings of Christ has both the Father and the Son.[17]

Your Word have I hid in my heart, that I might not sin against You[18] and Your blessings are on those that keep Your testimonies, and that seek You with their whole heart.[19] You are the God of my rock; in You will I trust: You are my shield, and the horn of my salvation, my high tower, and my refuge, my Savior: You save me from violence.[20] I will dwell in Your tent forever: I will trust in the shelter of Your wings.[21]

And now, Israel, what does the LORD your God require of you, but to fear the LORD your God, to walk in all His ways, and to love Him, and to serve the LORD your God with all your heart and with all your soul.[22]

And now, little children, dwell in Him; that, when He shall appear, we may have confidence, and not be ashamed before Him at His coming.[23] So remember, he that says that he dwells in Him ought to himself walk as Jesus did.[24]

REFERENCES

1) Psalms 15:1-5

2) Psalms 119:114

3) Psalms 27:5

4) Psalms 31:20

5) Psalms 25:14

6) Psalms 31:19

7) Psalms 71:3

8) Psalms 34:15

9) Psalms 4:3

10) Psalms 37:5

11) John 12:46

12) I John 4:15

13) John 14:16-17

14) John 15:4-7

15) I John 3:24

16) John 15:10

17) II John 1:9

18) Psalms 119:11

19) Psalms 119:2

20) II Samuel 22:3

21) Psalms 61:4

22) Deuteronomy 10:12

23) I John 2:28

24) I John 2:6

Chapter 2

YOUR CONFESSION

I will say of the LORD, "He is my refuge and my fortress: my God in Him will I trust." **Verse 2**

I will trust in the LORD with all my heart and not in my own understanding.[1] In all my ways acknowledging Him and He will direct my paths.[2] He is a shield to all that put their trust in Him,[3] and it is better to put trust in Him than to put confidence in man.[4]

I will not trust in my bow, neither will my sword save me.[5] When I am afraid, I will trust in You.[6] The LORD is on my side: I will not fear what man can do to me.[7] For the LORD is He that goes with me, to fight for me against my enemies, to save me:[8] And the LORD will utter His voice before His army, for His camp is very great and he that executes God's Word is strong.[9]

I will not fear, for God is with me: I will not be dismayed for He is my God: He will strengthen me: He will help me: He will uphold me with the right hand of His righteousness.[10] He is the Alpha and Omega, the beginning and the end.[11] He is the door: if any man enter by Him, he shall be saved.[12] He is the Good Shepherd, who gives His life for the sheep.[13] He is the Way, the Truth and the Life: No man comes to the Father except through Jesus Christ.[14] He is the vine and we are the branches: he that abides in Him and Him in them, brings forth much fruit; for without Him we can do nothing.[15] He is the one that lives and was dead and is now alive forever more.[16] For He is the LORD our God, the Holy One of Israel, our Savior.[17]

The LORD is my Rock and my fortress, my deliverer, my God and my strength.[18] He is good; His mercy is everlasting and His truth endures to all generations.[19] I will call upon His name[20] for the LORD is a great God[21] and He is high above all the people.[22] The name of the LORD is a strong tower; The righteous run into it and are safe.[23]

God's way is perfect; The Word of the LORD is tried; He is a shield to them that trust in Him.[24] He is my keeper[25] and my helper.[26] He is my peace,[27] my defense and the rock of my refuge.[28] He is great in power,[29] and able to make all grace abound toward me, so that in all things, at all times, I will have all that I need to abound in every good work.[30]

LORD, You will lead me in the way that I
should go,[31] because Your Word is a lamp
for my feet and a light for my path.[32] Indeed,
Blessed is the man that trusts in the LORD.[33]

REFERENCES

1) Proverbs 3:5

2) Proverbs 3:6

3) Proverbs 30:5

4) Psalms 118:8

5) Psalms 44:6

6) Psalms 56:3

7) Psalms 118:6

8) Deuteronomy 20:4

9) Joel 2:11

10) Isaiah 41:10

11) Rev. 1:8

12) John 10:9

13) John 10:11

14) John 14:6

15) John 15:5

16) Rev. 1:18

17) Isaiah 43:3

18) Psalms 18:2

19) Psalms 100:5

20) Psalms 105:1

21) Psalms 95:3

22) Psalms 99:2

23) Proverbs 18:10

24) II Samuel 22:31

25) Psalms 121:5

26) Hebrews 13:6

27)Ephesians 2:14

28) Psalms 94:22

29) Nahum 1:3

30) II Corinthians 9:8

31) Isaiah 48:17

32) Psalms 119:105

33) Psalms 34:8

Chapter 3

THE PROMISE OF DELIVERANCE

Surely He shall deliver you from the snare of the fowler and from the deadly pestilence.
Verse 3

Many are the afflictions of the righteous; but the LORD delivers him out of them all.[1] The LORD is my rock and my fortress and my deliverer; my God, my strength,[2] my high tower and my shield, in Him will I trust.[3] The righteous cry and the LORD hears and delivers them out of all their trouble.[4]

He delivers me from my enemies; yes He lifts me up above those that rise up against me.[5] He preserves the souls of the saints; He delivers them out of the hand of the wicked.[6]

You are my hiding place; You will preserve me from trouble; You will surround me with songs of deliverance.[7] The eyes of the LORD are upon them that fear Him, upon them that hope in His mercy,[8] to deliver

9

their soul from death and to keep them alive in famine.[9] He will fulfill the desire of them that fear Him: He will also hear their cry and will save them.[10]

The weapons of our warfare are not carnal, but mighty through God to the pulling down of strongholds;[11] Casting down imaginations and every thing that exalts itself against the knowledge of God and bringing into captivity every thought, to the obedience of Christ.[12] The LORD will keep him in perfect peace whose mind is stayed on Him because he trusts in Him.[13] Trust in the LORD forever for the LORD Jehovah is everlasting strength.[14]

God resists the proud but gives grace to the humble,[15] therefore humble yourself under the mighty hand of God, that He may exalt you in due time,[16] casting all your care upon Him for He cares for you.[17] Be sober, be watchful, because your adversary, the devil walks about as a roaring lion seeking whom he may devour.[18] Resist him steadfast in the faith.[19]

Be anxious for nothing, but in everything by prayer and supplication with thanksgiving, let your requests be known to God.[20] He will regard the prayer of the destitute and not despise their prayer.[21] The LORD hears the prayer of the righteous,[22] the prayer of the upright is His delight.[23] Be therefore sober and watch and pray[24] for the effectual fervent prayer of a righteous man avails much.[25]

The prayer of faith will save the sick and the Lord will raise him up; and if he has committed any sins, they will be forgiven him.[26] Hear my prayer, O God, give ear to the words of my mouth[27] and preserve my life from fear of the enemy.[28]

God is our refuge and strength, a very present help in trouble.[29] Persecutions and afflictions will come, but endure them, for the Lord will deliver you out of them all.[30] With God's love, you can bear all things, believe all things and hope all things.[31]

Be strong in the Lord and in the power of His might.[32] When the LORD is your strength, who is there to be afraid of?[33] Seek the LORD, His strength, and His face continually,[34] and He will be your strength and power, making your way perfect.[35] The eyes of the LORD run to and fro throughout the whole earth, to show Himself strong in the behalf of them whose heart is perfect toward Him.[36] Just wait on the LORD, and be of good courage and He will strengthen your heart.[37]

The Angel of the LORD will go before you[38] and encamp around you;[39] And the LORD will make the crooked places straight[40] and be with you, never failing you, neither forsaking you; so fear not, neither be dismayed[41] for the battle is not yours but God's.[42]

REFERENCES:

1) Psalms 34:19
2) Psalms 18:2
3) Psalms 144:2
4) Psalms 34:17
5) Psalms 18:48
6) Psalms 97:10
7) Psalms 32:17
8) Psalms 33:18
9) Psalms 33:19
10) Psalms 145:19
11) II Corinthians 10:4
12) II Corinthians 10:5
13) Isaiah 26:3
14) Isaiah 26:4
15) I Peter 5:5
16) I Peter 5:6
17) I Peter 5:7
18) I Peter 5:8
19) I Peter 5:9
20) Philippians 4:6
21) Psalms 102:17
22) Proverbs 15:29
23) Proverbs 15:8
24) I Peter 4:7
25) James 5:16
26) James 5:15
27) Psalms 54:2
28) Psalms 64:1
29) Psalms 46:1
30) II Timothy 3:11
31) I Corinthians 13:7
32) Ephesians 6:10
33) Psalms 27:1
34) I Chronicles 16:11
35) II Samuel 22:33
36) II Chronicles 16:9
37) Psalms 27:14
38) Exodus 32:34
39) Psalms 34:7
40) Isaiah 45:2
41) Deuteronomy 31:8
42) II Chronicles 20:15

Chapter 4

THE PROMISE OF PROTECTION

He shall cover you with His feathers, and under His wings shall you trust and find refuge: His truth and His faithfulness shall be your shield and buckler. **Verse 4**

Because you LORD have been my help,[1] in the shadow of Your wings I will make my refuge, until these calamities pass.[2] I will live in Your tent forever: I will trust in the shelter of Your wings.[3] You have also given me the shield of Your salvation and Your right hand holds me up.[4] My heart trusts in you, and I am helped; therefore my heart rejoices.[5]

Do not withhold Your tender mercies from me O LORD, let Your loving kindness and Your truth continually preserve me.[6] You will bless the righteous; with favor will You surround him as with a shield.[7] You O LORD are a shield for me, my glory and the lifter of my head.[8]

As for me, I will call upon God and the LORD will save me.[9] When I remember Him upon my bed and meditate on Him in the night watches, my soul will be satisfied and my mouth will praise Him.[10] LORD, you are my strength,[11] my rock and my fortress; therefore for Your name's sake, lead me, and guide me.[12]

When the Spirit of Truth comes, He will guide you in all truth.[13] All of God's commandments are truth,[14] and His Word is truth.[15] Jesus said of himself, "I am the Way, the Truth and the Life: no man comes to the Father except by Me."[16]

Let not mercy and truth forsake you; bind them about your neck; write them on the tablets of your heart,[17] so will you find favor and good understanding in the sight of God and man.[18] Let your heart retain my words: keep my commandments and live.[19] Get wisdom, get understanding: forget it not; neither decline from the words of my mouth.[20] The fear of the LORD is the beginning of wisdom: and the knowledge of the Holy is understanding.[21]

It is good to give thanks to the LORD,[22] to proclaim your love in the morning and your faithfulness at night.[23] Yes, great is your faithfulness,[24] that endures to all generations.[25]

The night is far spent and the day is at hand; let us therefore cast off the works of darkness, and put on the armor of light.[26] Put on the whole armor of God, that you may stand against the schemes of the devil.[27] For we do not wrestle against flesh and blood, but against principalities, against powers, against the rulers of the darkness of this world, against spiritual wickedness in high places.[28]

Put on the whole armor of God, that you may be able to withstand in the evil day and having done all, to stand.[29] Put the belt of truth around your loins and have on the breastplate of righteousness.[30] Have your feet shod with the preparation of the gospel of peace.[31] Above all, taking the shield of faith, with which you will be able to quench all the fiery darts of the wicked one;[32] And take the helmet of salvation, and the sword of the Spirit, which is the Word of God.[33] Pray at all times with all prayer and supplication in the Spirit and watching with all perseverance and supplication for all the saints,[34] and also pray that you may boldly open your mouth to proclaim the mystery of the gospel,[35] that you may declare it boldly.[36]

Remember, they that wait on the LORD, will renew their strength; they will mount up with wings as eagles; they will run and not be weary; they shall walk and not faint.[37]

REFERENCES

1) *Psalms 63:7*
2) *Psalms 57:1*
3) *Psalms 61:4*
4) *Psalms 18:35*
5) *Psalms 28:7*
6) *Psalms 40:11*
7) *Psalms 5:12*
8) *Psalms 3:3*
9) *Psalms 55:16*
10) *Psalms 63:6 & 5*
11) *Psalms 31:4*
12) *Psalms 31:3*
13) *John 16:13*
14) *Psalms 119:151*
15) *John 17:17*
16) *John 14:6*
17) *Proverbs 3:3*
18) *Proverbs 3:4*
19) *Proverbs 4:4*

20) *Proverbs 4:5*
21) *Proverbs 9:10*
22) *Psalms 92:1*
23) *Psalms 92:2*
24) *Lamentations 3:23*
25) *Psalms 119:90*
26) *Romans 13:12*
27) *Ephesians 6:11*
28) *Ephesians 6:12*
29) *Ephesians 6:13*
30) *Ephesians 6:14*
31) *Ephesians 6:15*
32) *Ephesians 6:16*
33) *Ephesians 6:17*
34) *Ephesians 6:18*
35) *Ephesians 6:19*
36) *Ephesians 6:20*
37) *Isaiah 40:31*

Chapter 5

THE PROMISE
OF COURAGE

You will not be afraid of the terror of the night:
Nor of the arrow that flies by day; Nor for the
pestilence that walks in the darkness; Nor for
the destruction that lays waste at noonday.
Verses 5 & 6

Be not afraid of the king of Babylon, of
whom you are afraid; be not afraid of him,
says the Lord: for I am with you to save
you, and to deliver you from his hand.[1]
Only rebel not against the Lord, neither fear
the people of the land; for they are bread for
you: their defense is departed from them
and the Lord is with you: fear them not.[2]

Hear O Israel, you draw near this day to
battle against your enemies: do not let your
hearts faint but fear not, and do not tremble
neither be terrified because of them; For the
LORD your God,[3] the LORD strong and
mighty, the LORD mighty in battle,[4] is He
that goes with you to fight against your enemies, to save you.[3]

Only fear the LORD, and serve Him in truth with all your heart; consider all the great things He has done for you;[5] and He will deliver you out of the hand of all your enemies.[6] The eye of the Lord is upon them that fear Him, upon them that hope in His mercy; To deliver their soul from death, and to keep them alive in famine.[7] Yes, the fear of the LORD is strong confidence,[8] and a fountain of life to depart from the snares of death[9] and prolong your days.[10]

God has not given us the spirit of fear; but of power, and of love, and of a sound mind.[11] So be strong, fear not: behold, your God will come with vengeance and divine retribution; He will come and save you.[12] Yes be strong and of good courage, fear not, nor be afraid of them: for the LORD your God is He that goes with you; He will not fail you nor forsake you.[13]

Be not afraid nor dismayed because of the vast army; for the battle is not yours, but God's.[14] Be of good courage and He will strengthen your heart, all you that hope in the LORD.[15] Yes, wait on the LORD: be of good courage and He will strengthen your heart: wait, I say on the LORD.[16]

The righteous are bold as a lion,[17] and will be remembered forever. He will not be afraid of evil tidings: his heart is fixed, trusting in the LORD. His heart is established, he will not be afraid, and in the end he will see his desire upon his enemies.[18]

Let not your heart be troubled: you believe in God, believe also in Me [Jesus].[19] My peace I leave with you, My peace I give to you, not as the world gives, so I give unto you.[20] When you lie down, you will not be afraid: yes, you will lie down, and your sleep will be sweet. Do not be afraid of sudden fear, neither of the destruction of the wicked when it comes. For the LORD will be your confidence, and will keep your foot from being taken.[21]

When I am afraid, I will trust in God.[22] I will not be afraid of what man can do to me.[23] Though I walk through the valley of the shadow of death, I will fear no evil: for You are with me; Your rod and Your staff they comfort me.[24] Though an army should encamp against me, my heart will not fear: though war should rise against me, even in this, I will be confident;[25] For the LORD is my light and my salvation; whom shall I fear? The LORD is the strength of my life; of whom shall I be afraid?[26]

But now says the LORD that created you, O Jacob, and He that formed you, O Israel, Fear not: for I have redeemed you, I have called you by name; you are Mine. When you pass through the waters I will be with you; and through the rivers, they will not overflow you: when you walk through the fire, you will not be burned, neither will the flame set you on fire.[27]

Let the weak say "I am strong",[28] and stagger not at the promise of God, through unbelief; but be strong in faith, giving glory to God, being fully persuaded that what He has promised He is able also to perform.[29] Do not cast away therefore your confidence, which has great reward,[30] but be confident of this very thing, that He which has begun a good work in you will perform it until the day of Jesus Christ.[31] So come boldly to the throne of grace, to obtain mercy, and find grace to help in time of need.[32]

Finally, my brothers, be strong in the LORD and in the power of His might,[33] stand fast in the faith, be men of courage,[34] and be strong in the grace that is in Christ Jesus.[35]

REFERENCES

1) Jeremiah 42:11
2) Numbers 14:9
3) Deuteronomy 20:3-4
4) Psalms 24:8
5) I Samuel 12:24
6) II Kings 17:39
7) Psalms 33:18-19
8) Proverbs 14:26
9) Proverbs 14:27
10) Proverbs 10:27
11) II Timothy 1:7
12) Isaiah 35:4
13) Deuteronomy 31:6
14) II Chronicles 20:15
15) Psalms 31:24
16) Psalms 27:14
17) Proverbs 28:1
18) Psalms 112:7-8
19) John 14:1
20) John 14:27
21) Proverbs 3:25
22) Psalms 56:3
23) Psalms 56:11
24) Psalms 23:4
25) Psalms 27:3
26) Psalms 27:1
27) Isaiah 43:2
28) Joel 3:10
29) Romans 4:21
30) Hebrews 10:35
31) Philippians 1:6
32) Hebrews 4:16
33) Ephesians 6:10
34) I Corinthians 16:13
35) II Timothy 2:1

Chapter 6

THE PROMISE OF SAFETY

A thousand shall fall at your side and ten thousand at your right hand; but it will not come near you. You will only watch with your eyes as you witness the reward of the wicked. **Verses 7 & 8**

My son, keep sound wisdom and discretion, and they will be life to your soul, and grace to your neck. Then you will walk on your way safely and your foot will not stumble. When you lie down, you will not be afraid; yes, you will lie down and your sleep will be sweet.[1] For whoever listens to Wisdom will live safely and shall be quiet without fear of harm.[2]

The fear of man brings a snare: but whoever puts his trust in the LORD shall be safe.[3] For the name of the LORD is a strong tower: The righteous run into it, and are safe.[4] Indeed, the LORD is my rock, and my fortress, and my deliverer; my God, my strength, in whom I will trust; my buckler, and the horn of my salvation, and my high tower.[5]

A horse is a vain thing for safety: neither shall he deliver any by his great strength,[6] though the horse is prepared against the day of battle: safety is of the LORD.[7] So make God your refuge and fortress,[8] placing all your trust in Him,[9] and you will live in safety,[10] preserved from trouble,[11] surrounded by mercy,[12] guarded by angels,[13] sheltered from the storm and shaded from the heat.[14]

Call upon Him in the day of trouble, and He will come to your defense, be your refuge,[15] hide you in His pavilion, set you upon a rock,[16] calm the storm and bring you to your desired haven.[17] During troubled times, He will be with you and honor you,[18] for His thoughts for you are precious, and great is the sum of them.[19]

Where no counsel is, the people fall: but with many counselors there is safety.[20] Hold me up LORD, and I will be safe: and I will have respect for Your statutes continually.[21] For You store up sound wisdom for the righteous, and You are a shield to them that walk uprightly.[22]

The LORD sees the oppression of the poor and hears the sighing of the needy and says "Now I will arise, I will set him in the safety he longs for."[23] Yes, the Lord makes my feet like the feet of a deer, and sets me securely upon high places.[24]

REFERENCES

1) Proverbs 3:21-24
2) Proverbs 1:33
3) Proverbs 29:25
4) Proverbs 18:10
5) Psalms 18:2
6) Psalms 33:17
7) Proverbs 21:31
8) Psalms 91:2
9) Psalms 4:5
10) Psalms 4:8
11) Psalms 32:7
12) Psalms 32:10
13) Psalms 91:11
14) Isaiah 25:4
15) Psalms 59:16
16) Psalms 27:5
17) Psalms 107:29-30
18) Psalms 91:15
19) Psalms 139:17
20) Proverbs 11:14
21) Psalms 119:117
22) Proverbs 2:7
23) Psalms 12:5
24) Psalms 18:33

Chapter 7

THE PROMISE
OF SECURITY

Because you have made the Lord your refuge and the most High your place of dwelling; There shall no evil befall you, neither shall any plague come near your tent. **Verses 9 & 10**

Know this, that in the last days perilous times will come.[1] In the world, you will have tribulation: but be of good cheer; I [Jesus] have overcome the world.[2] I will never leave you nor forsake you,[3] I am with you always, even unto the end of the world.[4]

The LORD saves His anointed; He will hear him from His holy heaven with the saving strength of His right hand.[5] The angel of the LORD encamps all around them that fear Him, and delivers them,[6] for the salvation of the righteous is of the LORD.[7]

My defense is from You God[8] and in the shadow of Your wings I will take refuge, until these calamities be over.[9] You are the strength of my salvation, covering my head

27

in the day of battle,[10] indeed, a very present help in trouble.[11]

The LORD is my light,[12] my strength, my shield,[13] my confidence,[14] my rock and my defense.[15] Therefore, my foot will not be snared,[14] my heart, which trusts in You, will greatly rejoice,[13] I will never be shaken,[15] and I will fear no evil.[16]

We were called to fellowship with God's Son, Jesus Christ our Lord,[17] and truly our fellowship is with the Father, and with His Son, Jesus Christ,[18] who is not ashamed to call us brothers.[19] However, if we say that we have fellowship with Him, and walk in darkness, we lie, and are not living the truth: But if we walk in the light, as He is in the light, we have fellowship with each other, and the blood of Jesus Christ His Son cleanses us from all sin.[20]

The LORD will hear you in the day of trouble; the name of the God of Jacob will defend you,[21] yes, He will defend you from them that rise up against you.[22] No evil will happen to the just[23] and whoever keeps the commandment will feel no evil thing,[24] but the wicked will be filled with trouble.[23]

The way of the LORD is strength to the upright,[25] therefore I will go in the strength of the LORD, making mention of His righteousness,[26] for in the day when I cried, He answered me, and strengthened me with strength in my soul.[27]

Now the God of hope fill you with all joy and peace in believing, that you may abound in hope, through the power of the Holy Ghost,[28] And may the peace of God,[29] the grace of our Lord Jesus Christ, the love of God, and the communion of the Holy Ghost, be with you all. Amen.[30]

REFERENCES

1) II Timothy 3:1
2) John 16:33
3) Hebrews 13:5
4) Matthew 28:20
5) Psalms 20:6
6) Psalms 34:7
7) Psalms 37:39
8) Psalms 7:10
9) Psalms 57:1
10) Psalms 140:7
11) Psalms 46:1
12) Psalms 27:1
13) Psalms 28:7
14) Proverbs 3:26
15) Psalms 62:2
16) Psalms 23:4
17) I Corinthians 1:9
18) I John 1:3
19) Hebrews 2:11
20) I John 1:7
21) Psalms 20:1
22) Psalms 59:1
23) Proverbs 12:21
24) Ecclesiastes 8:5
25) Proverbs 10:29
26) Psalms 71:16
27) Psalms 138:3
28) Romans 15:13
29) Romans 15:33
30) II Corinthians 13:14

Chapter 8

THE PROMISE OF HELP

For He will give His angels charge over you, to keep you in all your ways. They will lift you up in their hands, lest you dash your foot against a stone. **Verses 11 & 12**

Behold, God is my helper and ally;[1] Yes my help comes from the LORD, who made heaven and earth,[2] who rides through the heavens to my help in His majestic glory through the sky.[3]

Though I walk in the midst of trouble, You will revive me: You will stretch forth Your hand against the wrath of my enemies, and Your right hand will save me.[4] When I cried to you in times past, You answered me, and strengthened me in my soul.[5] When this poor man cried, You LORD heard me, and saved me out of all my troubles.[6]

O taste and see that the LORD is good: blessed is the man that trusts in Him.[7] The LORD will help them, and deliver them: He will deliver them from the wicked, and save

them, because they trust in Him.[8] For the
LORD your God is He that goes before you,
He will fight for you against your enemies,
to save you.[9]

Behold, the eye of the LORD is upon them
that fear Him, upon them that hope in His
mercy; To deliver their soul from death, and
to keep them alive in famine.[10] For the steps
of a good man are ordered by the LORD:
and He delights in his way. Though he fall,
he will not be utterly cast down: for the
LORD upholds him with His hand.[11] So,
pray without ceasing and in everything give
thanks: for this is the will of God in Christ
Jesus concerning you.[12]

Cast your burden upon the LORD, and He
will sustain you: He will never permit the
righteous to be shaken.[13] For the LORD
your God in the midst of you is mighty; He
will save, He will rejoice over you with
gladness; He will rest in His love, He will
rejoice over you with singing.[14]

Men ought always to pray, and not to
faint;[15] For the eyes of the LORD run to and
fro throughout the whole earth, to show
Himself strong in the behalf of them whose
heart is perfect toward Him.[16] Indeed, God
is our refuge and strength, an ever present
help in trouble,[17] Let us therefore come
boldly to the throne of grace, that we may

obtain mercy and find grace to help in time of need.[18]

There are many that say of me, "There is no help for him in God." But you, O LORD, are a shield for me; my glory, and the lifter up of my head. I cried unto the LORD with my voice, and He heard me out of His holy hill. I laid down and slept, I awakened for you had sustained me. I will not be afraid of ten thousands of people, that have encamped themselves against me all around. Arise, O LORD; save me, O my God: for you have struck all my enemies on the cheek bone and broken the teeth of the ungodly.[19]

Be pleased, O LORD, to deliver me: O LORD, make haste to help me;[20] For I am poor and needy, yet You LORD, think about me: You are my help and my deliverer; Do not delay O my God.[21] Let Your hand help me; for I have chosen Your precepts.[22]

Our help is in the name of the LORD,[23] and because He has been my help, I will rejoice in the shadow of His wings,[24] for God has power to help, and to cast down.[25] Remember, the Angel of the LORD encamps all around them that fear Him and each of them He delivers.[26]

REFERENCES

1) *Psalms 54:4*
2) *Psalms 121:2*
3) *Deuteronomy 33:26*
4) *Psalms 138:7*
5) *Psalms 138:3*
6) *Psalms 34:6*
7) *Psalms 34:8*
8) *Psalms 37:40*
9) *Deuteronomy 20:4*
10) *Psalms 33:18-19*
11) *Psalms 37:23*
12) *I Thess. 5:17-18*
13) *Psalms 55:22*
14) *Zephaniah 3:17*
15) *Luke 18:1*
16) *II Chronicles 16:9*
17) *Psalms 46:1*
18) *Hebrews 4:16*
19) *Psalms 3:2-7*
20) *Psalms 40:13*
21) *Psalms 40:17*
22) *Psalms 119:173*
23) *Psalms 124:8*
24) *Psalms 63:7*
25) *II Chronicles 25:8*
26) *Psalms 34:7*

Chapter 9

THE PROMISE
OF VICTORY

*You will tread upon the lion and the cobra: the
young lion and the serpent you will trample
under foot.*   **Verse 13**

I can do all things through Christ which
strengthens me,[1] because greater is He that
is in me than he who is in the world.[2] For
whatever is born of God overcomes the
world and this is the victory that overcomes
the world, even our faith.[3]

Many are the afflictions of the righteous,
but the LORD delivers him out of them all.[4]
So rejoice not against me, O my enemy, for
when I fall, I will arise; when I sit in darkness, the LORD will be a light to me.[5]

The steps of a good man are ordered by the
LORD: and He delights in his way.[6] Though
he fall, he will not be utterly cast down; for
the LORD upholds him with His hand.[7] For
a just man falls seven times, but rises up
again; but the wicked shall fall into calamity,[8]

and they shall soon be cut down like the grass and wither as the green herb.[9]

The salvation of the righteous is of the LORD: He is their strength in time of trouble.[10] He shall subdue the people under us and the nations under our feet.[11] Through Him we will push down our enemies; through His name we will tread them under that rise up against us.[12] These things I have spoken to you, that in Me you might have peace.[13]

Behold, I give you power to tread on serpents and scorpions and over all the power of the enemy; and nothing will by any means hurt you.[14] Nay, in all these things we are more than conquerors through Him that loved us.[15]

I am persuaded that neither death nor life, nor angels, nor principalities, nor powers, nor things present, nor things to come,[16] nor height, nor depth, nor any other creature will be able to separate us from the love of God, which is in Christ Jesus our Lord.[17]

Thanks be to God who gives us the victory,[18] and always causes us to triumph in Christ,[19] who having spoiled principalities and powers, He made a show of them openly triumphing over them in it.[20]

Submit yourselves therefore to God. Resist the devil, and he will flee from you.[21] Do not be overcome with evil, but overcome evil with good,[22] resisting steadfast in the faith, knowing that the same afflictions are accomplished in your brothers that are in the world.[23] Remember, that if you faint in the day of adversity, your strength is small.[24]

REFERENCES

1) Philippians 4:13
2) John 4:4
3) I John 5:4
4) Psalms 34:19
5) Micah 7:8
6) Psalms 37:23
7) Psalms 37:24
8) Proverbs 24:16
9) Psalms 37:2
10) Psalms 37:39
11) Psalms 47:3
12) Psalms 44:5
13) John 16:33
14) Luke 10:19
15) Romans 8:37
16) Romans 8:38
17) Romans 8:39
18) I Corinthians 15:57
19) II Corinthians 2:14
20) Colossians 2:15
21) James 4:7
22) Romans 12:21
23) I Peter 5:9
24) Proverbs 24:10

Chapter 10

THE PROMISE OF HONOR

Because he has set his love upon Me, therefore I will deliver him. I will set him on high because he has known My name. He will call upon Me and I will answer him: and I will be with him in trouble; I will deliver him, and honor him.
Verses 14 & 15

But now says the LORD, them that honor Me I will honor, and they that despise My Word shall be lightly esteemed;[1] And whoever despises My Word shall be destroyed: but he that respects the commandment will be rewarded.[2] Know therefore that the LORD your God, He is God, the faithful God, which keeps covenant and mercy with them that love Him and keep His commandments to a thousand generations.[3]

Promotion comes neither from the east, nor from the west, nor from the south. But God is the judge: He puts down one and raises up another.[4] The fear of the LORD is the beginning of wisdom,[5] and wisdom is the principal thing; therefore get wisdom: yes, with all your effort get wisdom. Exalt her, and she will promote you: she will bring you to honor, when you embrace her.[6] Those that seek her early will find her.[7]

You should love the LORD your God with all your heart and with all your soul, and with all your might.[8] And it will come to pass, if you listen diligently to the voice of the LORD your God, to observe and to do all His commandments, that the LORD your God will set you on high above all nations of the earth.[9]

They that know God's name will put their trust in Him; for the LORD has not forsaken them that seek Him;[10] For He has said, "I will never leave you nor forsake you."[11] In fact, the people that do know their God will be strong, and do exploits.[12] So give thanks unto the LORD, call upon His name and make known His deeds among the people.[13]

The LORD is good, and ready to forgive; and plenteous in mercy unto all them that call upon Him.[14] So call upon Him in the day of trouble and He will answer you[15] and deliver you, and you will glorify Him.[16] Yes, the LORD is near unto all them that call upon Him, to all that call upon Him in truth.[17] For whosoever shall call upon the name of the LORD shall be saved.[18] Therefore I will call on the LORD, who is worthy to be praised: so shall I be saved from my enemies.[19]

Keep yourselves in God's love as you wait for the mercy of our LORD Jesus Christ to bring you into eternal life,[20] knowing that all things work together for good to them that love God, to them who are the called according to His purpose.[21] For this is the love of God, that we keep His commandments: and His commandments are not grievous.[22] For I am persuaded that neither death, nor life, nor angels, nor principalities, nor powers, nor things present, nor things to come, nor height, nor depth, nor any other creature shall be able to separate us from the love of God, which is in Christ Jesus our Lord.[23]

Behold, I give unto you power to tread on serpents and scorpions, and over all the power of the enemy: and nothing shall by any means hurt you.[24] Remember, humble yourselves under the mighty hand of God, that He may exalt you in due time.[25]

REFERENCES

1) I Samuel 2:30
2) Proverbs 13:13
3) Deuteronomy 7:9
4) Psalms 75:6-7
5) Psalms 111:10
6) Proverbs 4:7-8
7) Proverbs 8:17
8) Deuteronomy 6:5
9) Deuteronomy 28:1
10) Psalms 9:10
11) Hebrews 13:5
12) Daniel 11:32
13) I Chronicles 16:8
14) Psalms 86:5
15) Psalms 86:7
16) Psalms 50:15
17) Psalms 145:18
18) Romans 10:13
19) II Samuel 22:4
20) Jude 1:21
21) Romans 8:28
22) I John 5:3
23) Romans 8:39
24) Luke 10:19
25) I Peter 5:6

Chapter 11

THE PROMISE OF LIFE

With long life will I satisfy him, and show him My salvation. **Verse 16**

I call heaven and earth to record this day against you, that I have set before you life and death, blessing and cursing; therefore choose life, that both you and your seed may live.[1] To be carnally minded is death; but to be spiritually minded is life and peace.[2]

For the law of the Spirit of life in Christ Jesus has made you free from the law of sin and death,[3] And if Christ be in you, the body is dead because of sin; but the Spirit is life because of righteousness.[4] For if by one man's offense death reigned through that man; how much more will those who receive God's abundant provision of grace and of the gift of righteousness reign in life,[5] and unto eternal life through the one man, Jesus Christ.[6]

This is life eternal, that they might know you, the only true God and Jesus Christ whom you have sent.[7] For God so loved the world that He gave His only begotten Son, that whoever would believe on Him, would not perish, but have everlasting life.[8] Jesus said, "I am the Way, the Truth, and the Life; no man comes to the Father except by Me."[9]

He that believes on the Son has everlasting life and he that believes not the Son shall not see life but the wrath of God abides on him.[10] Because straight is the gate and narrow is the way which leads to life and few are they that find it.[11] He that finds his life will lose it and he that loses his life, for My sake, will find it.[12] For even the Son of Man came not to be served, but to serve and give His life as a ransom for many.[13] In Him was Life and the Life was the Light of man.[14]

Blessed is the man that endures temptation, for when he is tried he will receive the crown of life that the Lord has promised to them that love Him.[15] He that will love life and see good days, let him refrain his tongue from evil and his lips from speaking guile.[16] A wholesome tongue is a tree of life, but perverseness in it crushes the spirit.[17]

He that guards his mouth guards his life, but he that opens wide his mouth will have ruin.[18] Remember, death and life are in the power of the tongue.[19] My son, be attentive to my words,[20] for they are life to those that find them and health to all their flesh.[21] For whoever finds wisdom, finds life and will obtain favor of the LORD.[22]

For what is your life? It is a vapor, that appears for a little time and then vanishes away.[23] Therefore I say to you, Take no thought for your life, what you will eat or what you will drink; or for your body, what you will wear. Is not your life more than food and your body more than clothes? Seek first the kingdom of God and His righteousness and all these things will be added to you.[24]

Jesus said, "I am the bread of life: he that comes to Me will never hunger and he that believes on Me will never thirst."[25] He only is my rock and my salvation; He is my defense; I will not be greatly moved.[26] He brought me up out of a horrible pit, out of the miry clay, and set my feet upon a rock,[27] and He has put a new song in my mouth.[28] He will show me the path of life.[29]

This is the record, that God has given to us eternal life, and this life is in His Son.[30] He that has the Son has life; and He that has not the Son of God has not life.[31] These things I have written to you that believe on the name of the Son of God; that you may

know that you have eternal life, and that
you may believe on the name of the Son
of God.[32]

REFERENCES

1) *Deuteronomy 30:19*

2) *Romans 8:6*

3) *Romans 8:2*

4) *Romans 8:10*

5) *Romans 5:17*

6) *Romans 5:21*

7) *John 17:3*

8) *John 3:16*

9) *John 14:6*

10) *John 3:36*

11) *Matthew 7:14*

12) *Matthew 10:39*

13) *Mark 10:45*

14) *John 1:4*

15) *James 1:12*

16) *I Peter 3:10*

17) *Proverbs 15:4*

18) *Proverbs 3:13*

19) *Proverbs 18:21*

20) *Proverbs 4:20*

21) *Proverbs 4:22*

22) *Proverbs 8:35*

23) *James 4:14*

24) *Matthew 6:25, 33*

25) *John 6:35*

26) *Psalms 62:2*

27) *Psalms 40:2*

28) *Psalms 40:3*

29) *Psalms 16:11*

30) *I John 5:11*

31) *I John 5:12*

32) *I John 5:13*

Chapter 12

HOW TO OBTAIN REAL LIFE

God's desire for every person is to enter into the life that He offers. If you would like a new start on life, read these seven pointers and respond sincerely from your heart. You will not be disappointed.

I. Our Sinful Condition

Like sheep, we have all gone astray; we have turned every one to his own way[1] and sinned, with all of us falling short of the glory of God.[2]

II. The End Result Of Sin

Sin, when it is finished its course, brings forth death,[3] and the reward or wages of sin is death.[4]

III. What God Did About It

God loved the world so much, that He gave his one and only Son that whoever would believe in Him, would not perish, but have life everlasting.[5] Yes God demonstrated His great love for us, in that while we were yet sinners, Christ died for us.[6]

IV. How We Can Respond To God's Offer

If you will confess with your mouth the Lord Jesus, and will believe in your heart that God has raised Him from the dead, you will be saved. For with the heart man believes unto righteousness; and with the mouth confession is made unto salvation.[7] As many as receive Him to them He gives power to become the sons of God.[8]

V. Our Promised Assurance

For I am persuaded, that neither death, nor life, nor angels, nor principalities, nor powers, nor things present, nor things to come, nor height, nor depth, nor any other creature shall be able to separate us from the love of God which is in Christ Jesus,[9] [who himself said...] "I will never leave you nor forsake you,"[10] and, "lo, I am with you always, even unto the end of the world."[11]

VI. Our New Walk

I urge you brothers, by the mercies of God, that you present your bodies a living sacrifice, holy, acceptable unto God, which is your reasonable service. And do not be conformed to this world: but be transformed by the renewing of your mind.[12]

VII. Above All Else

The most important commandment of all is this: You should love the Lord your God with all your heart, and with all your soul, and with all your mind, and with all your strength.[13]

REFERENCES

1) Isaiah 53:6
2) Romans 3:23
3) James 1:15
4) Romans 6:23
5) John 3:16
6) Romans 5:8
7) Romans 10:9-10
8) John 1:12
9) Romans 8:38-39
10) Hebrews 13:5
11) Matthew 28:20
12) Romans 12:1-2
13) Mark 12:29-30

A PRAYER

Father God,

*I acknowledge that I have sinned
and fallen short of your glory.*

*All my good works to obtain
righteousness are as filthy rags.*

*I believe that Jesus died for me
and that you raised Him from
the dead to live forever.*

*I ask You to forgive me
of all my sins and to give me
this free gift of eternal life
through Jesus Christ.*

Amen.

ADDITIONAL RESOURCES

The Bible Incorporated

A pocket-sized compilation of Scripture in easy to understand, conversational style addressing 101 mostly work and business topics. Over 300,000 sold.

Grace for Grief

A daily devotional for the first year of grief. Rather than teach about grief, this book attempts to comfort others with the same comfort we received in the loss of our children.

Words In Red—The Teachings of Christ Compiled

A pocket-sized compilation of the greatest teachings of Jesus Christ, arranged by topic. Discover His teachings again—for the first time in this powerful collection.

Michael & Brenda Pink...

Have written or co-written over a dozen books. Brenda is an artist, specializing in oil paintings that celebrate life. Michael is the author of *Selling Among Wolves—Without Joining The Pack!* He trains individuals and corporations in Biblical principles for succeeding in sales. *For information, contact him at www.SellingAmongWolves.com.*